FRAGMENTS

Written By:
Elaine Martin Uonelli

Elaine M. Uonellé
aka Domino

FRAGMENTS

You are about to read a collection
of thoughts inspired by experiences,
special occasions, given situations,
and unique people.

It's time to sit back, relax, and
leave the realities of the moment.

The following excerpts are complete
unto themselves, and are not
necessarily related to one another.

Elaine Martin Vonelli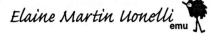

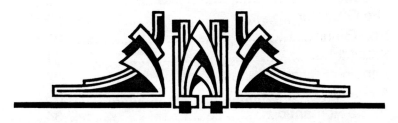

Contents

"TIME"

It has been said that time is
relevant. If you are waiting,
a minute seems an hour. If
you are trying to complete a
task in a limited time frame,
an hour seems but a minute.

LOOK TO THE PAST

Imagine yourself
    In years gone by...
Another time
    Unknown to mankind.

A climate for growth
    Of unknown things;
Of dinosaurs
    That ruled this wild land.

Untamed and unbowed,
    Those fierce dinosaurs
Each was unique
    Each one stood proud.

Imagine the earth
    A swamp marsh;
Footsteps were left,
    Embedded in stone.

Imagine the earth
    A desert land...
Feeding a host...
    Then dry dust and bones.

Pre-history times...
  A distant past
Shrouded in mist
  and different climes.

Now open the gates
  of those closed minds.
Broaden their scope,
  Let spirits soar.

From centuries past
  and yesteryears gone.
Events in those days
  impinge on today.

THEN & NOW

Monday—laundry,
Gather up the clothes,
Whites and colors—
Separate the loads.

Scrub boards, rinse tubs,
Wringers on machines;
Stretchers, clothespins,
Hang clothes on the line.

Blowing, drying,
In the breeze so fair.
Take down, fold up,
Bring into the house.

Sprink'ling—starching,
Mangles and hot irons,
Smoothing, pressing
Now to put away.

Wash day, what day?
Any day you choose;
Full load, half load
Separate the clothes.

Hot-cold cycles,
Choose with utmost care.
Washers, dryers
Let them do their chores.

Fluff up, shake out,
Fold or hang on rods.
Closets, dressers,
Now to put away.

SO WE WAIT

Printed in Great Poems of
The Western World, Vol. II
World of Poetry Press (1990)

Traffic jam up. . .
So we wait; so we wait.
Christmas Sale Rush -
So we wait; so we wait.

Friend or mate
In a meeting;
So we wait; so we wait.

Looking for
that special seating
So we wait; so we wait.

Waiting rooms. . .
So we wait; so we wait.
Airport mix-up. . .
So we wait so we wait.

Jury's Out.
A verdict pending . . .
So we wait; so we wait.

At a park
Or at a bank ---
Lines and lines;
So we wait; so we wait.

Labor pains ---
A baby's coming
So we wait; so we wait.

At a deathbed---
Loved one dying;
So we wait; so we wait.

What's to come
From all this waiting?
Is it patience?
Just frustrating?

Spent a lifetime---
Waiting, waiting.
Is it worth it?
So we wait; so we wait.

NOSTALGIA

Do you remember when...
When there was such a thing
As a building 'specially meant
To fill prescription needs?

Not only was it quaint,
A meeting place it was,
Where townsfolk often went
To satisfy their needs.

While waiting for their script,
They might sit down awhile;
A soda fountain treat
Could tempt the sourest soul.

The years have come and gone,
And now an owner new
Replaced the pills and vials
With memorabilia.

A meal we may consume,
Relive those bygone days,
Enjoy camaraderie,
And talk about the past.

WORLD IN MOTION

Back and forth
The pendulum swings;
Tick tock. Tick tock.

Sands of time
Are running out;
Tick tock. Tick tock.

Time goes on...
Never ceasing;
Tick tock. Tick tock.

Tides will ebb,
And tides will flow;
Tick tock. Tick tock.

No one stems
The passing time;
Tick tock. Tick tock.

Changing seasons;
World in motion;
Tick tock. Tick tock.

TIME OF SPRING

Looking at the blue sky,
Feeling the cool breeze,
Listn'ng to the wind chimes,
Doing what you please.

Tasting fresh picked berries,
Smelling fresh cut grass,
Riding in the country,
Rivers smooth as glass.

Finding broken eggshells
From a family new,
Hungry baby robins
Touched by morning dew.

Sowing seeds and planting,
Watering the field,
Weeding out intruders,
Waiting for the yield.

Heeding all around you,
Treasuring your finds,
Sights and sounds of springtime
Waken dormant minds.

LIVE FOR TODAY

Take time to smell the flowers,
Don't worry 'bout tomorrow,
Live for the day...
Don't dwell on sorrow.

I'm glad to take a pain-free breath,
To move about at will,
To be in charge of all my life...
Develop any skill.

Find some good in every day,
Be positive in thought,
Let the hurts fall by the way—
We find what has been sought.

A NEW MILLENNIUM

Away with the old,
Not only a year—
A whole century
Is gone, now that's clear.

Forget not the past,
So much has been gained,
Inventions tested,
Fame sought and attained.

Ideas rampant,
And theories unclaimed,
Discoveries made,
New knowledge is gained.

A century new—
'Tis the 21st,
What is in store?
Adventurers thirst.

Thirst for more knowledge,
Insatiable quest,
Look to the future—
There's no time to rest.

"PEOPLE"

People we meet play a part
in our lives. They may
influence our thoughts and
our actions through what
they have said, or through
what they have done.

Some people have a positive,
uplifting effect on others.
Some people have a negative,
down-grading effect.

There are people we want
to remember and those we
want to forget.

What would the world be
were there no people?

The Doctor Who Loved STONES

I knew a doctor once who had an obsession with stones. Now any general practitioner is concerned about stones when they form in the kidney or gall bladder of his patients. When I say this doctor loves stones, I am talking about natural rock formations in nature. In the last few years he has surrounded his home and clinic with stones he has collected.

The doctor's wife says, "Once my husband sees a stone that really appeals to him, he literally moves heaven and earth to obtain it. It is not unusual for him to locate a paticular stone and wait 3 or 4 years, until it can be accessible to him. I've seen him, single-handedly, use a long board as a lever to pry a large stone loose and get that same stone onto a borrowed pick-up. I still don't know how he does it! Even a medium-sized stone is heavy; just try to lift one!"

The stones are various sizes, shapes, colors, etc. you could say they are arranged in an impressionistic style. The doctor placed the stones to his own satisfaction.

Many of the stones were transferred from the doctor's boyhood home. These stones bring back memories of the first time he and his dad found them and placed them.

It would be difficult to select any one particular stone as a favorite; each stone is unique and has its own individuality. The family's pet poodle favors certain stones, but even he appears at a loss to choose, at times, because of the large variety available.

The doctor offers advice to anyone lifting or placing stones..."Be sure you know how to handle the stones so you don't injure yourself. Sometimes it is best to hire a professional."

TRIBUTE TO MOTHERS

A mother gives us life,
And eases all our hurts;
We often take for granted
The selfless love she gives.

We grow up all too soon,
And leave her tender care;
No gratitude is shown
For sacrifices made.

Adulthood we pursue,
Establish our own homes,
Our contact may be rare—
No time to pay our due.

Before we know, she's gone,
As dawn gives way to night.
We pray that she did know
She's loved forevermore.

THE MAN WHO REVERED MOTHER

There was a man we knew,
We met him just by chance.
Knowing him, we loved him...
Our life he did enhance.

His home was like a shrine;
Built lovingly by hand...
Of river stone 'twas made;
On solid rock, not sand.

His faith in God and man,
His architecture showed...
For patterns in the stone,
Depicted heaven's road.

A canopy of stars
Adorned his mother's bed,
Designed for beauty rare,
Where she might rest her head.

Her virtues he extols;
Her purity untouched.
Memories are cherished...
To him she meant so much.

A PERFECT MATCH

He came from across the sea,
Straight from old Italy.
No stick in the mud was he—
The world he wanted to see.

He traveled west by railroad car.
He saw the world—both near and far.
He worked hard and saw a lot—
Wisdom grew; experience wrought.

All this time was she—
Waiting home for that special he.
At last they met, and two hearts set,
They wed and raised a family.

Inspired by the life of my in-laws.

A TRIBUTE TO HAIR STYLISTS

Creative hands, say some;
Hackers, shout others;
Goals set to satisfy
Changing fads and trends.

Women are demanding;
Men are much the same;
Wanting a make-over
In vanity's name.

Alter length and color;
Make the straight hair curl;
Sophisticated style—
Or simple—as you will.

Look to the hair stylist;
Trust her judgment call;
Experience she has
To know what's best for all.

ONE

Bone of my bone,
Flesh of my flesh,
How deep goes the bond?
Two hearts not yet met.

Out from the past
You did emerge,
How great was your love
To never forget?

But just a child,
Such a great load,
To bear in your heart
This mem'ry grown old.

Others may judge,
But who are they?
Were they in your place?
Should they have a say?

Time has a way
To lessen pain,
But now you're complete—
The lost has been found!

THE COLLECTORS

A fascinating group...
Restrictions have they none.
Collectors one and all—
They do it just for fun.

They search both near and far
To find that which they seek,
What treasures may abound
In discards where they peek?

For them there is no end
To searching for their prize,
Garage sales yield rewards
To unsuspecting eyes.

The objects of their search
Comprise most anything...
From knives to dolls to cars—
To teddy bears and rings.

An endless chain they form,
As on and on they search,
They're running out of space!
Oh where, oh where to perch?

OUTSIDE LOOKING IN

The Amish have a way of life
Promoting peace and shunning strife.
They labor in their farm and field,
A hoe and scythe they know to wield.

Clothing styles and colors set,
Their teaching, preaching, all well met.
Appliances, 'lectricity,
Within their homes you will not see.

A phone and auto are taboo,
They even wear a special shoe.
A buggy and a horse convey
The folks to meetings far away.

The modern ways are not for them,
Though progress all around does hum.
A simple style of living choose,
Accepting only certain views.
They share the burdens, toils of life
With fam'ly, friends, and neighbors strive.

From them we could a lesson learn—
Tradition we should never spurn.
Respect for others' way of life,
Avoiding all that leads to strife.

Shackled by the bonds of love,
Desired no other way,
They basked in sunshine,
Weathered storms,

That crossed the path they trod.
Together raised a family,
Bridged the gap of old and young,
Perpetuate their line.

Homemaker, wife, mother was she;
Breadwinner, husband, father, he.
Both were tender, caring, giving,
Thought of self left far behind;

Forged a chain that can't be broken,
Withstood the test of time.
Enduring love had these soul mates,
A marriage made in heaven;

Sixty years together shared,
Sustained by understanding.
Youthful passions years may cool,
True friendship lasts forever;

Tired bodies give up life,
But spirits linger on,
Join with mem'ries of the past
To shield the one not gone.

TRIBUTE TO VOLUNTEERS

You are the volunteers,
Unsung heroes all,
You lighten all our load,
Answering our call.

Could we do our job—
Never does it end,
Without the able help
You so freely lend?

Selfless human beings,
Seldom saying no,
You are another hand,
Add an extra glow.

Bending 'neath our burden,
Flexing with the chore,
Smiles that help to brighten,
Make our spirits soar.

Worth we cannot measure,
Words cannot describe
Our appreciation,
Which we'll never hide.

Little can we offer,
Simple words at best,
Gratitude and thanks,
Warm feelings in our breast.

OPRAH WINFREY

O utreach stretches 'cross the nation
P hilanthropic are her deeds
R eading and the arts she fosters
A ctive in her search for truth
H onored by her zealous fans

W insome smile draws people to her
I nternationally acclaimed
N urturer of souls and spirits
F riendly gestures toward her guests
R ecognized and adulated
E yes hold visions—vast their range
Y esterdays become tomorrows

A TRIBUTE TO OUR FIREFIGHTERS

Professionals—they heed our call
When we express our need;
They're trained to battle raging fires,
To quell inferno's will.

Dedicated to their task,
Relentless their assault
On flames that would devour,
They risk both life and limb.

Intimidated? No, not they,
Our firefighters brave,
Appreciate the job they do,
And all the lives they've saved.

Give honor to our firefighters,
Respect them as they toil,
Support them in their arduous fight,
And grieve when lives are lost.

A single parent in this world,
One can't help but admire,
That special bond 'tween parent-child,
Who's raised by one not hired.

The hardships faced nobody knows,
To meet the basic needs,
The parent fights to raise the child,
Unnumbered are the deeds.

Encouragement this parent gives,
Who nurtures every day,
This child for whom there's so much love,
Who's never in the way.

This parent's pride cannot be hid
When speaking of the child,
Extolling all accomplishments,
Done in the child's own style.

THE EDUCATOR

Once in a lifetime
You may meet someone
Honest and sincere—
Know him if you can.

Dedicated, true
To the work he chose,
He'll not deviate
From the plan he knows.

Where is such a one?
Few may recognize,
Admire and respect
His views as such a prize.

Such a privilege,
Working side by side,
Sensitivity
Cannot be denied.

(Inspired by: My Principal, John Weiss)

BOB EVANS

B orn to make a difference

O wns a restaurant chain

B old is his commitment

E arned his recognition

V alued by his patrons

A ttuned to public tastes

N othing did deter him

S urmounted obstacles

What magic is there in this world
That brings two souls together?
The tie that binds forevermore,
Both good and bad times weathered.

This time on earth so quickly flies,
Life's thread so soon spins out,
Yet know our time is only lent,
There is no room for doubt.

The man and woman now unite,
Two hearts that beat as one,
Not always tuned to other's mind,
Yet open ere all's done.

Now joined throughout eternity,
The fam'ly gathers round
To honor and to reminisce,
Their voices loud resound.

DANCING FRENZY

Sedate they are when on the job,
Demure is their demeanor,
Stresses of the day build up,
Quenching buoyant spirits.

Eve'ning comes and they're released,
Shed their inhibitions,
Time to loosen up and roll—
Rocking with the rhythm.

A FRIEND

How many things
Can tongue or pen
Begin to tell—
What is a friend?

Let's make a list...
A friend is one
Who sees our best
And overlooks our faults.

A friend is there
In time of need;
Who's standing by
Through thick and thin.

A friend can give
A list'ning ear,
Or lend
A helping hand.

A friend gives us
Encouragement;
A friend
Will understand.

To be a romantic...
'Tis truly a curse.
So many around us...
Belong in a hearse.

Clinical! Sterile!
Leave feeling behind;
Thoughts scientific...
No room for our kind.

Our thoughts other worldly,
In a world war-torn, berated.
Fantasies abound...
In the world our minds created.

Who can share these thoughts?
A breed of men, apart
From the ebb and flow,
As seen in nature's chart.

To balk at nature's plan,
And be at odds with others;
Leave stark reality...
Believe in men as brothers.

Yet time and time again
Our fondest hopes and dreams
Are dashed against the rocks
By those around with schemes.

Perhaps someone, somewhere,
Can understand our call.
Reach out! Span time and space,
We are human, after all.

Is there anyone among us who has never had a dream? Either we have a dream of reality, or a dream of fantasy.

Millions of people have dreams...very few are willing to sacrifice, or have the perseverance it takes to make their dreams come true.

Once there were two teenagers who had a dream. Their dream was to build a trimaran to sail around the world. These two boys launched a project you would have to see to believe! After three years of toil and setbacks, the boat was 70% completed.

The design and workmanship on the craft were due, to a great degree, to the creativity and ingenuity contributed by the two dreamers. Of course certified marine engineers supplied the basic plans.

Everywhere you turn today someone has his hand out for a donation to some cause or another. These young men have not solicited for financial aid. Their work was delayed because they had to take time away from their project to earn money toward its continuance.

This awesome project was completed after five additional years. The launching, to date, has yet to take place.

And so the dream lives on...

FROM AN ADOPTED CHILD

I am "special,"
Don't you see?
My mom and dad...
Both picked me!

Childless they were,
Not content...
A son they sought;
Efforts spent.

What did they find?
Lucky me!
A daughter for
Their family.

For when they looked
Upon this babe,
She smiled up
From where she lay.

Love did bloom
That very day,
She was theirs
Without delay.

KISMET

I met a man with second sight;
It was a chance encounter.
Adept at reading tarot cards,
His gift did make one wonder.

A first impression was amiss,
To think him ordinary.
A conversation yielded up
A most unusual story.

Who knew he was a psychic rare;
The spiritualist path he chose?
Belief in angels' miracles,
His love he shares unbidden.

He reaches out a helping hand
To those who need uplifting.
Advice he offers anyone
Whose mind and heart is open.

A kinship sprang up instantly;
How strange and fascinating
To bond with one of variant views,
Yet still have much in common.

by Elaine M. Uonelli
Sept., 2003

When he was but a boy,
He used to like to climb
Up trees and poles, on roofs,
The feeling was sublime.

When he became a youth,
The mountain peaks he hailed,
Undaunted by the height
Of skyscrapers he scaled.

Now fully grown is he,
A roofer's job he took,
Today he tops the trees,
Atop a crane he looks.

The view he does enjoy,
When at an awesome height,
Adventure he does seek,
He'd love to soar in flight.

The day was much brighter
   When we did meet,
Upon that summer morn.

Our face to face meeting
   Was just by chance—
Or was it preordained?

One soul found another,
   Our lives entwined,
A joining of the minds.

So rare a discov'ry,
   A friendship formed,
Defying the distance.

By blood not related,
   Sisters at heart,
Poetic verse we share.

Support we can offer
   In letter form,
We vent our joys and woes.

BEHIND THE SCENES

Who are the unsung heroes
We oft forget to name?
Quietly they stand aside,
While others garner fame.

Look around and you will see
Some folks who blend right in;
Look at who is on the job,
Unnoticed in the din.

Employed for public service,
These folk we value not,
Should they not be at their post,
We'd note an empty spot.

Meshing, guiding, pave the way,
Completing what they start,
Enhancing tasks of others—
A necessary part.

Can you name these special souls?
Or where they may be found?
Hidden jewels amid the field,
By duty are they bound.

TO INCORRUPTIBLE LAWYERS

Attorneys-at-law,
Among the elite
Who tread courthouse halls.
You might chance to meet—

A woman or man,
His counsel will lend;
A privilege rare,
To name one as friend.

In lives of mankind
There oft comes a time
When problems arise
That need legal minds.

Advice giv'n when sought
Has value untold;
When given a friend,
Its worth's above gold.

A lawyer must search
His mind and his books,
Interpret the law,
Evaluate looks.

It's no easy task
To answer all quests;
He seeks and he finds,
To pass every test.

BUTTERFLY WOMEN

Why do we choose the butterfly
To clip into our hair,
To dangle from our pierc'ed ears,
To pin onto our shirt?

Our fascination with this 'sect
Stems from its colors bright;
It drinks its fill from nectared blooms
And flits from flower to flower.

Its graceful moves attract our eyes,
A glider in full flight,
Adjusting to the moods of wind,
Attuned to fragrant scents.

Some pin these beauties for display,
Collectors ever seek—
But we would rather view them live,
Unhindered in their quest.

And so we search for replicas
Of gentle butterflies—
Accessories adorn
And add a nature's touch.

WE MET SANTA CLAUS

We met Santa Claus
At an unlikely spot-
Snug Harbor 'twas the place,
The eve'ning-it was hot.

Disguised in reg'lar garb,
His beard gave him away,
His modulated voice
Would soothe the wildest stray.

Table talk was great,
A winsome smile and face
Created happy thoughts-
Negated time and space.

Devoted to his role,
His cause he did pursue,
To make a happier time
For many or for few.

A man who's recognized
By the discerning few-
How fortunate were we
When he was in our view.

THE CHOSEN FEW

We are the lefties in this world;
Oh, where can we be found?
Just look around and you will find
We're few, and don't abound.

Unique our writing strategy—
First print is oft reversed.
We slant our hand or paper so;
For this we have rehearsed.

The brain is right side dominant,
Confusing left and right
We plan ahead to chart our course—
To keep a line of sight.

Now baseball touts the rare southpaw;
His value is proclaimed.
From right hand players point of view,
He may appear untamed.

Our world designed for right handers,
Unending challenge gives;
A lefty quickly must adapt,
For that's the way he lives.

THE DOWNFALL OF MAN

There is a fine line between good and evil. The magnetic pull of evil is strong, and too often leads man to step over the line.

It is so much easier to yield to anger and to thoughtless acts than to abide by the Golden Rule. Man is often controlled by his base instincts, making him capable of horrendous deeds.

Some men successfully battle the war between good and evil. The continuous struggle to do what is right is often perceived as weakness. In truth, these are the men with character. We can rely on them to be steadfast.

MAN'S INHUMANITY TO MAN

I'll never understand
Man's inhumanity
To fellow human beings,
Deserving to be free.

Our hist'ry books are filled
With numerous accounts
Of perpetrated deeds
Against another soul.

What right has any man,
To give him so much power
O'er other human lives—
To smite them down in spite?

The settlers did attack
All tribes of Indians;
To reservations forced,
Deprived of game and land.

From Africa they came,
Against their right and will;
Enslaved to rich white men,
Accepting what befell.

A civil war and strife
Between the North and South;
A travesty to pit
A brother 'gainst his brother.

The Germans did believe
The lies that Hitler told
Against the Jewish race—
Extermination reigned.

Al Qaeda is allied
With Taliban support
To spread a terror far
Infecting all the world.

Oh, where does this all end?
As long as hate and fear
Are rampant in men's hearts,
Injustice will prevail.

CLOSURE - SEPTEMBER 11, 2001

Respect for human life—
Oh, where can it be found,
When terrorists abound,
Who strike down with a knife?

The weapons they may choose
Are guns or knives or bombs.
Who knows where they'll attack,
Or whose lives will be lost?

Fanatics are they all—
Intent to back their cause.
They will not be contained,
Obeying someone's call.

The leader is insane
To harbor so much hate.
He'd sacrifice his own,
So much has he to gain.

Conceived a heinous plot;
Attacked our nation's own,
Supported by his band.
We pray they will be caught.

The retribution's real.
We must protect our land
From terrorists at large,
Their mission now revealed.

ACCELERATE

Accelerate; accelerate;
Acceleration is...
Our nation's passion.

Accelerate; accelerate;
Throw caution to the wind.
In and out of traffic
Keeping in the lead.

Where could they be going?
Respect for fellowman
Is left outside the door.

Accelerate; accelerate;
No patience for the plodder.
Disregarding speed signs,
Radar detectors on.

All the hustle bustle,
All the broken laws;
Possible destruction...
And now a red light.

AGGRESSION

Aggression...aggression...
I'm on my way now,
I'm here to stay now—
Without delay.

Aggression...aggression...
I'm pushing onward,
I won't be floundered,
Out of my way!

Aggression...aggression...
Often tailgating,
Cannot 'bide waiting,
Making my way.

Aggression...aggression...
Highways and road rage,
Disregard speed gauge,
Forging ahead.

Going on a lion hunt,
Tiger hunt, panther hunt—
Going on a big game hunt
To see what I can see.

Looking for an elephant,
Crocodile, chimpanzee—
Want to take some photographs
To keep in memory.

Going on a leopard hunt,
Rhino hunt, tortoise hunt—
Going on a big game hunt—
Just you and me.

Looking for a diamond back,
Antelope, ocelot—
Want to take some videos
So we can see—

Animals both wild and free;
Living free, running free.
Animals that we'll protect
From mad humanity.

Inspired by humanity's destructive habits.

EXCESSES

Let's keep on smoking—
Our lungs to defile.
Let's keep on drinking—
Our reflexes lose.

Let's keep on drugging—
Our brains we can fry.
Let's keep on eating—
Make bodies awry.

Let's keep on speeding—
Raise accident tolls.
Let's keep on warring—
Our lives we snuff out.

Let's keep on killing
Our animal friends;
Endanger species,
Reduce ratios.

Let's keep polluting
The air that we breathe,
The water, the land,
'Til all life will end.

"DEATH"

Death is not a pleasant subject. It is, however, inescapable, and something each person must deal with in his or her own way.

Death may result from natural causes or an accident. It may also be the result of violence---self-inflicted, as in suicide, or perpetrated by another, as in homicide.

Death may bring with it a saddness for our loss, or a release from suffering.

Death may touch our lives through a relative, a friend, an acquaintance, someone we have read or heard about, or even a family pet.

Unnatural Causes

An innocent child, an abusive adult...
A tragic ending.

A little girl, on her way to school,
Is waylaid, raped, and murdered.

A teen wants to experience
A new adventure with drugs...
Ends up on a slab.

Young people seeking a thrill,
Taking a dare...
Flirting with death,
And ending up dead.

A partygoer takes one for the road,
And ends up in the morgue.

Trying to beat that train...
Defying death.

Self-inflicted...
Embracing death.

Slain by another...
Overcome by death.

In the wrong place at the wrong time...
Seeking life, but finding death.

Precious life; no turning back...
What a waste! What a waste!

GRIEF

If you have ever lost someone or something near and dear to you, you have experienced grief.

As a child, I had sorrowed for dead pets. As I matured, I was able to sympathize when others lost their loved ones.

The depth of grief varies. When my father died, I felt the ultimate grief. At that time I did not try to put feelings into words.

Now that God has called my mother home, I am experiencing grief anew. I tried to analyze the characteristics of grief and came to the conclusion that it acts upon us as the ocean. There are calm periods---we are in control and are relatively untroubled. Then the waves begin--far out--building and building, until we are overcome. As the waves recede, a measure of tranquility is restored. How thankful I am for those calm periods! I believe they are God's way to help us heal our hearts.

I share these thoughts with you, the reader, in the hope they may be comforting to you in your time of grief.

Tajah
The "Crown Royale" (India)

Printed in The Golden Treasury of Great Poems
World of Poetry Press (1989)

"It's just another dog," they said.
But no, that's just not true.
Our Tajah was much more than that...
Much more to me and you.

He came into our home to stay,
About five years ago today.
He made us laugh; he made us cry.
He was such a cute little guy!

Our Tajah loved to play and run.
He loved to sit out in the sun.
He loved to cuddle close to you;
Especially when you're feelin' "blue."

He was not "just another dog;"
Oh, no! Not our little Tajah!
We all loved him so.

Emergency—
Sirens wailing,
Life flight ready,
Distraught loved ones.
Hospital primed,
Staff alerted,
Intravenous
Drips and needles,
Respirators
Activated,
Crash carts ready
Just in case.
Accidents or
Nat'ral trauma,
Life is slipping
Through the hourglass.
Time stands still for
All in waiting;
Death is hov'ring,
Patient, silent.
Motionless, the
Victim suffers,
Brain engaged but
Not responding;
Vultures gath'ring
For the harvest.

ON THE LIGHT SIDE

The humorous side of
life is what keeps us
going. Many serious
events can be viewed more
objectively at a later date.
A situation that is far from
funny at the time it
occurred, may have a
humorous overlay in
the future.

Sometimes another person
is instrumental in helping
us to see the comic side of
our life. Is the glass half
empty or half full? It
depends on your outlook.

Try writing a humorous
epitaph, such as "They
say you can't take it with
you, so I tried to spend it
all before I went!"

BALANCE

Looking for a joke,
Play on words at best,
Ferret out the meaning,
All is said in jest.

Try to find the humor
Hidden in the words,
Know the double meanings,
Adjectives or verbs?

Overcome the mys'try,
Understand the plot,
Laughter often follows,
Once the tale is out.

Comedy is vital,
Equalizes stress,
Balances equations,
Makes us more—not less.

SOMETHING LOST

Oh, to lose a penny...

What a terrible thought!

It won't buy you a thing,

But, it can save you a lot.

For loss of that one cent,

Now you must cash a bill.

It surely wasn't meant...

For you to lose that cent!

AN ORDEAL

My dentist worked for the gestapo...
Of that I have no doubt;
For when I sit deep in his chair,
I nearly scream and shout.

My teeth he cleans so thoroughly,
And when at last he's done,
It takes a week to recuperate...
Believe me---it's no fun!

He picks and pokes to find a hole,
Ev'ry probe I feel.
Alas, he is successful...
Now there's more to my ordeal.

"Give me novocaine," I cry,
"I cannot stand the pain!"
"Of course, my dear," says he with a smile,
And injects my gums with saline?

I swear it's naught but a placebo;
It doesn't touch the pain.
Who does he think he's kidding?
Does he think I'm not totally sane?

Air, drill, water, spit,
Will this go on forever?
He doesn't stop to let me breathe...
He thinks he's really clever!

Put the clamp on, suction in;
Strangel, gag, choke, cough...
Come on doctor, have a heart!
Now he wants to talk!

Filling's in now; let's relax.
Don't jut your jaw out so.
That wasn't bad, don't you agree?
I hurry up to go.

Another torture I've withstood;
I shake in disbelief.
Can I survive another year...
Just to keep my teeth?

SEQUEL

To this little poem I wrote,
I now must add a verse...
For I have found a dentist new,
Who is not like the first.

My dentist has two extra hands,
An assistant trained
To smooth the way and help allay
The stress that I've contained.

The former writ, I must admit,
Still speaks of current fears.
And yet there's hope, to help me cope...
There's progress through the years!

TIME LAPSE

It's not because I'm older,
Nor dread senility;
It couldn't be Alzheimers
That makes my mem'ry flee.

There are a few occasions
My mind seems put on hold;
I stand in contemplation—
A purpose to unfold.

What was I now just doing?
Why am I standing here?
I find myself reviewing
The possibilities.

Sometimes I am successful,
Recalling what I need;
Sometimes my steps are wasted,
My mind...it did recede.

It's not because I'm older,
Nor Alzheimer's disease,
My brain's in overload mode,
Confusing thoughts and deeds.

A TRIBUTE TO NOODLES

Oodles of noodles—
How very mundane.
Oodles of noodles—
A pleasant refrain.

Oodles of noodles-
A basic for meals.
Oodles of noodles—
A lifetime of deals.

Oodles of noodles—
All sizes and styles.
Oodles of noodles—
Bring forth many smiles.

Oodles of noodles—
We boil in a pot.
Oodles of noodles—
We eat while they're hot.

Oodles of noodles—
With sauce or with cheese.
Oodles of noodles—
They're sure to please.

Oodles of noodles—
We're here to receive
Oodles of noodles—
Our hunger relieved.

Converse with scotch tape?
You're out of your mind!
What lengths it will go—
Refusing to bind.

Outrageous its whims,
Wrecks havoc on nails,
My temper is frayed,
How loud are my wails!

Recalcitrant child
This obstinate tape—
Adheres where it will,
Clings fast—loses shape.

Tenacious its hold
On roll and on me;
Refuses to stick—
From packages flees.

My brain it doth seethe,
My blood it doth boil,
My patience long gone—
Continue this toil?

Temptation to toss
This tape in the trash,
Give up in disgust—
But let's not be brash.

Curses I stifle,
Must wait lest I scream;
Restore peace of mind
And try once again.

CELEBRATE

Another birthday we've survived;
Now aren't we glad to be alive?

Our joints may stiffen up a bit;
Our memory may tend to flit.

A few pounds added here and there—
That's something we would like to share!

Each day we count a blessing rare,
A sense of humor helps us bear
The arrows and the slings of life,
And we've survived the daily strife.

If we could have a smile a day,
Our troubles would be kept at bay.

SIGNIFICANCE OF PETS

It has been documented that pets, especially cats and dogs, prolong life. The combination of dependency and independence works magic on the owners. All kinds of creatures provide inspiration for stories and poems. Is it their similarity or diversity that appeals to humans? Entertaining antics and heroic deeds often reach the media and are dispersed to the public in newspapers, over the radio, or on the television. There are those who have dedicated their lives to the preservation of endangered species. Others are aligned with shelters or prevention of animal cruelty.

DINOSAUR HUNT

Tramp, tramp, tramp, tramp,
All day long...
Looking for a dinosaur,
None to be found.

Dig, dig, dig, dig,
All day long...
Looking for a dinosaur,
None in the ground.

Dive, dive, dive, dive,
All day long...
Looking for a dinosaur,
None in the sound.

Where are the dinosaurs?
Where have they gone?
Have to try another day...
Maybe in that mound.

Clunk, clunk, clunk, clunk,
Hear that sound?
Looking for a dinosaur...
See what I found?

Bones, bones, bones, bones,
All around,
Bones of dinosaurs...
In the mound.

To the museum,
That's where I'll go.
dinosaur bones...
I'll take to show.

A SHELL'S TALE

My first home was in the salt water.

I loved to look at all the beautiful
colors of the sea creatures and
plants around me. I loved to listen
to the swishing sound of the water.

I felt happy and secure, until one
day a giant sea turtle swallowed
me. It was dark and mysterious
inside the turtle. I was so scared!

I thought the darkness would last
forever, but the next thing I knew,
the sea turtle choked, and spit me
out. I was happy to be back in my
world. I hid in a huge bunch of
sea anemones.

I wonder what "tales" other objects
or creatures could share if they
were able to speak.

The Shark --- Friend Or Foe?

When you see a shark,
What goes through your mind?
Is it to be feared?
Is it ever kind?

Something to respect---
That we can't deny.
Knowledge of its kind;
Know the reason. Why?

Ruthless man-eater
Is the great white shark.
Gentle plant-eater
Is the huge whale shark.

Oh, how vile a crime
Humankind has wrought,
Overlooking good---
Killing without thought!

Science has begun
To appreciate
Facets of the shark,
To which we can relate.

Think before we act.
Know the good from bad;
Lest we find our ourselves
Losing all we had.

INVASION

Our house was taken over.
Who or what could it be?
An alien from outer space?
Perhaps the huge Godzilla.

A biker gang gone wild?
The Creature from the Black Lagoon?
The ancient, fearsome Mummy,
Or Big Foot on the loose?

What horror was in store for us?
What dreadful fate awaited?
Could we escape the spell?
But no—it mesmerized us.

What enslaved us by its power?
No one would ever guess.
A feline's captivation
Had tamed us like the rest.

SAGA OF A SHELL

Recorded on Sound of Poetry
The National Library of Poetry (1998)

Washed upon the shore;
Crushed into the sand;
What a cruel end...
Tides brought me to land.

From a sheltered start,
Looking far ahead...
To a future grand,
On my ocean bed.

Many sights to see...
Dream world, colors bright;
Awesome shapes and sounds...
All my world alight.

Unbeknownst to me,
Lurked a fate unkind...
Creatures from the deep
Found me as I dined.

One caught me in its jaws,
Took me from my place,
Dragged me to its cave,
Left me there to waste.

Currents underground
Loosed me from my jail,
Forced me out and up...
What a fearsome gale!

Caught up in a wave;
Carried to the shore;
Here at last I lay,
Lost forevermore.

Nothing else remained...
Hope left far behind;
Then a child found me...
Now my future shined!

A FELINE'S DILEMMA

The lure of ladders
 I cannot resist,
To climb to the top
I need to desist.

A view from on high,
I'm queen of the world,
Of all I survey
The mys'try's unfurled.

I am in control
Until I return,
The ground is so far,
Oh, when will I learn?

The way going up
Is simple at best,
The way going down
Puts one to the test.

The choice now is mine,
To backtrack or jump,
A tough decision,
Now's no time to slump.

I look for a place
To take off and land,
I spring for a leap,
The space I have spanned!

THE SEEKER

What's that tapping
At the window?
Tap, tap, tapping
Without stopping?

To the window,
What is out there?
Eyes are looking;
Now rewarded.

Brilliant cardinal,
Shelter seeking,
Tap, tap, tapping
To gain entry.

Seed is set out
For the taking;
Sustenance free;
Bird surviving.

INSTINCT

Declawed I may be,
But never deterred,
Back nails are intact—
Retracted and sheathed.

When need does arise
Sharp claws will emerge
To offer purchase
When leaving my perch.

Unfortunate she,
My mistress at rest—
I leap off her lap
And dig into flesh.

My claws rake her thigh,
She yelps out in pain,
Examines her wounds,
Discomfort will wane.

No blame laid on me,
Can I be accused—
Intending to maim?
Just list' to my mews.

Victim, my mistress,
Collateral damage—
My instinct prevails—
Loosed, on a rampage.

Tamed— but yet feral,
Inherited traits
Emerge now and then—
Law of the jungle.

GUARDED

Its eyes are black onyx,
Unblinking, alert;
Its ears are antennae
That no sound may skirt.

Its body is upright,
On haunches it rests;
In prayer paws are raised
'Gainst its quivering breast.

A nervous demeanor,
A restless brown tail,
On guard against danger—
Poised—ready to sail—

Away from the sunflowers
And birdseed it eats,
It flies through the branches—
To safety retreats.

DISAPPEARING ACT

Into the house I raced,
Preceded by my catch;
A chipmunk fled my hold,
De-clawed, I could not snatch.

The creature ran and hid
Behind the furniture;
How wise this little beast,
Not yielding to my lure.

With paws outstretched I reached
To bring the chipmunk in,
The wily creature moved,
Escaped behind a bin.

How brazen is this 'munk,
It walked out on the floor,
It perched atop the couch,
But could not find the door.

Defeated for a time,
Pursuit is now at bay,
I wait for my next chance,
Perhaps another day.

ESCAPE

Out of the doorway,
Sneaky was I.
Rapid and wily,
Now I could fly.

Boun'dries can't hold me,
Go where I will,
Enjoy my freedom,
Getting my fill.

Stomach's now growling,
Time to return,
Come, let me in now,
Dinner I've earned.

Sitting and waiting
Impatiently,
Watching and list'ning,
Where's family?

Fine'ly the headlights
Beam in the drive,
No hesitating,
Now I'm alive!

A FINICKY CAT

Did you ever hear
Of a finicky cat,
Who eats none of this,
But will eat some of that?

The ears will perk up
When the op'ner meets can,
Appearance is prompt
To check out the off'ring.

A paté once pleased,
But taste buds have altered;
One sniff and she's off,
Rejecting the dish.

Let's try something new,
The fish is disgusting,
Yet kitty accepts
When it's fresh from the tin.

Don't dare to repeat
A serving too often,
Or kitty turns tail,
And stalks off in disdain.

WAITING GAME

Here I sit upon my perch,
Immobile as can be,
Not a muscle will I move,
My discipline's the key.

Patience adds to my appeal,
What creature could resist?
Tail is still, no whisker twitch—
I blend into the mist.

Birds unwary come to feed,
I'm ready for the pounce,
Nothing can escape my clutch,
No matter how they flounce.

Come to me my feathered friends,
I'm harmless—can't you see?
View me not as other cats,
I wouldn't hurt a flea.

As I reach out for my prize,
Prepared to seize my prey,
Mistress now on the alert,
And hits me with the spray.

THE LURE OF FLIGHT

Eyes look up at the blue skies above and watch the
birds swoop, dive, and glide—lifted by the wind
and propelled by their wings. Envy stirs in the
breast of man—he wants to emulate this wild
freedom, unfettered by the bounds of earth.
Intense observation of our aviary friends led inven-
tive men to construct an artificial means to reach
the heavens.

Who could imagine the first simple, often
unsuccessful flying machines would evolve into
spaceships, capable of leaving earth's gravitational pull?

The Call

Come hurry now—
Let's take a vow;
To Oshkosh we will go.

By air or land,
We'll join the band,
To see an awesome show.

Let's spread our wings—
We'll join with kings,
The grounds we will explore.

Come fly away
To EAA,
And have a
wondrous day.

PHEASANT RUN

To Pheasant Run we'll go,
To view a big display—
Chuck's airplanes in a row;
We'll have a fun-filled day.

They're ready to be flown;
To reach an awesome height;
They're Chuck Reed's very own—
They are a wond'rous sight.

These pampered planes are clean,
The Warbirds now are gassed,
They're ready to be seen,
And flown aloft at last.

Then down again they come,
The ride was super great,
The hangar talk does hum,
Let's hurry, don't be late.

Inspired by Pheasant Run Airplane Museum
Owned by Charles & Gretchen Reed

OUR VANISHING PIONEERS

We came upon a lovely pair
One sultry summer day.
They manned a booth at EAA,
A message to relay.

By "M" and "M" we know them now—
Their dedication rare,
They represent Lawsonomy;
No efforts do they spare.

Their faces glow from inner light,
As Lawson's deeds they share.
Their tireless pioneering talks
They give most anywhere.

Enthusiasm is their stamp
For what they do proclaim—
A principle to guide our lives,
In Alfred Lawson's name.

Now Margie's entered heaven's gates;
Her "Good Reactions" peal.
Her partner, Merle, is left behind
To carry on their zeal.

A MAN—ALFRED LAWSON

There was a man—
A fine upstanding kind of man.
He proved himself in many ways,
Through his days,
To make the world a better place.
But who does know—
What he has done
In sports and flight, there's only one.

The first airlines
He did conceive.
A great airline
To meet the people's need.
But who does know—
What he has done?
He sought not fame,
And sacrificed all monetary gain.

A credit plan—
He did propose;
He spread the word abroad.
"Equality," he said, "for ev'ry man."
But who does know—
What he has done?
Lawsonomy—
Should fall from ev'ry tongue.

Inspired by learning of A. Lawson through
M & M (Merle & Margie Hayden)

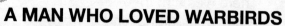

A MAN WHO LOVED WARBIRDS
Printed in The Compass (April, 1989)
Confederate Air Force / Missouri Chapter

A graveyard for airplanes!
Who heard of such things?
Yet stretched out before us...
Were countless wrecked wings.

These glorious warbirds
Once flew, oh so proud;
With many a vict'ry,
No need for a shroud.

Alas, when their time came,
Shot down in their prime,
Few cared for past glories...
'Twas truly a crime!

Made utterly useless,
No more could they fly.
Abandoned and helpless...
To rust and to die.

Then came there a man,
Concerned by their plight.
All was not lost now...
For them he would fight!

With flatbed and truck,
And chain did he come.
He bargained for hours;
At last things did hum!

His belov'd warbirds
Were brought home to rest;
Their dignity honored,
Brought peace to his breast.

RELEASE

Cycles, sailboats, planes and autos,
Horses, zebras, burros, camels
Offer freedom to the rider,
Commonplace or the exotic.

May appeal to few or many,
Stress relievers, soothe the spirit,
View the world from different angles,
Alter attitudes and bias.

Provide solitude from chaos,
Recreation, pleasure boundless,
On road or sea, in field or air,
Mount your steed—enjoy the moment,
All too soon return to earth.

OUR SPIRITUAL SIDE

Throughout the history of man there are times he seeks answers to questions that he has no background to investigate. Indeed, ere are still many instances when science, logical thought and reasoning are unable to bridge the gap. Once a man succumbs to the idea that he did not create himself, nor is he in control over phenomena in nature, health issues, etc. he turns to a divine/spiritual explanation. Giving supernatural powers to God or gods provides an answer to those questions that have no answer. Faith, trust, belief in something or someone outside the human realm satisfies the quest for otherwise unattainable knowledge.

THE SPIRITUAL SIDE OF CHRISTMAS

Christmas—the season of giving,
Even as God gave His son,
That we might have life everlasting,
If only we trust and believe.

Unselfish He offered His life,
Mankind He wished to redeem,
Cleansing the heart and the spirit,
That we, unblemished might be.

Purified by His blood,
Our sins are washed away,
Enabling us to tread
The heavenly path He paved.

Apart from hustle and bustle,
And shopping in the stores,
Apart from all the glitter,
Take time to thank our Lord.

TO THE ZEALOTS

I have respect for your belief,
Please have respect for mine;
Your dedication and your zeal
I can't help but admire.

I only wish I had the time
To contrast and compare
Interpretations of the Word
As translated by man.

Be not deceived, you cannot sway
A man whose mind is set;
Convinced you are of what is right,
Conflicting views arise.

You fill a need for those lost souls
Who suffer and who seek,
Who know not what can fill their need.

Perhaps a word from you
Can redirect the path they've chose—
Enlightenment from dark.

It's well to keep an open mind,
To look beyond yourself;
Enhance those truths that you've been taught,
And question—what is right?

I BELIEVE

Our world today is so complex,
We don't know right from wrong;
Which road to take along the way—
Bereft amid the throng.

Brought up in rules of righteousness;
The Bible as our guide;
Beset by scientific laws,
Which tenet should abide?

The atheist, he knows what's true;
Agnostics say they're right.
The skeptic comes along,
And scoffs at all in sight.

What does it matter after all,
Who's right or who is wrong?
Will truth prevail, no matter what?
Can we just trail along?

Yet I believe a higher power
Directs our destiny,
Giving us the right to choose...
Creator...Master...He.

"INTROSPECTION"

Some writings come
from our own observations
or deep, personal feelings.

How do you see yourself?
Your own self concept?
An interesting exploration--
don't you think?

AM I A POET?

Am I a poet?
Surely you jest!
I'm not a poet;
I can't pass the test.

A poet is special,
A poet works hard,
Dedicated to write,
Is truly a bard.

To works of a poet
I can't compare,
I can't compete
With one who's so rare!

I have no style,
No set pattern formed,
I don't follow rules,
My works would be scorned.

I do try to rhyme,
Words come from my heart.
I try to conform,
But, where do I start?

My writing's compulsive
Not planned and thought out,
Though sometimes
I struggle for words,
There's no doubt.

I don't go for length;
Brevity is my pleasure;
To write what I feel,
And to share with whomever.

Who understands
A mind so complex
As that of a poet,
Who makes the words flex?

Dare I join the ranks?
Be included as one?
Or am I a counterfeit
Out for some fun.

Can you bear with this fledgling?
Be understanding and kind?
Reach out and accept
The thoughts from my mind.

I never aspired
To the heights poets reach;
Their thoughts are not mine...
There's no room for speech.

Perhaps, in a small way
I now dare admit
I share your spirit,
Your soul and your wit.

And, so in the end
No more words fall.
Am I a poet
After all?

emu

PURPOSE

Can you say you never
Looked into a mirror,
Asked the age-old question,
What purpose have I here?

Do not be alarmed,
This is nothing new,
Doubts are not uncommon,
In life we often rue...

Goals we did not reach,
Change what might have been,
Things we did not do,
Places left unseen.

Just appreciate
What you are and have,
People's lives you've changed
With a helping hand.

Focus on good deeds,
Letting failures fade,
Remaining on the path
You yourself have laid.

Peace of mind will follow,
If you reconcile
All your heart's desires,
Life you'll find worthwhile.

A WISH

A wish, a wish,
If granted one wish,
What would you wish for?

Money and fame?
A castle in Spain?
Would these satisfy?

A lasting wish
Or temporary?
What do you want?

A wish for self,
Or for another?
Confusion doth reign.

Would you choose wealth,
Or would you choose health?
There's always world peace.

Personal needs,
And your desires,
Dictate what you wish.

Lasting effects
May arise from your wish.
Beware what you wish.

APPRECIATE

Appreciate! Appreciate!
Appreciate yourself
And the world you live in.
Appreciate who you are,
What you are,
The things that only
You can do.

It isn't always good;
It isn't always bad;
But look on the sunny side,
Away from the darker side,
And you will know you're special---
You're one of a kind!

GIVEN A CHOICE

In today's world,
Given a choice,
Would you choose sight?
Would you choose sound?

What can you see?
Colors so bright.
What can you hear?
Soft sounds at night.

What can you see?
Books that abound.
What can you hear?
Background of sound.

What can you see?
Obstacles near.
What can you hear?
Warnings so clear.

Precious is sight.
Precious is sound.
Don't make us choose,
It's too profound!

DAYDREAM

Daydream, daydream,
All I do is daydream.
Daydream, daydream,
All day long.

Wake up, wake up,
Time for me to wake up.
Wake up, wake up,
Hear this song.

Listen to the message.
Open up my ears.
Open up my mind
And broaden all my spheres.

Time for daydreams,
Not instead of list'ning.
Listen, think,
And find my way.

DESTINY

If we give up on the dreams and miracles of life, what is left? Far too many people face the harsh realities of life, and have little comfort or hope to sustain them. The family structure has broken down in so many homes— leaving the child(ren) to contend with an uncertain future concerning his/her caregivers.

Some turn to alcohol and/or drugs to obtain a temporary release from the undesirable aspects of daily life. The far-reaching effects of these potentially lethal substances do not begin to justify their use, which can only result in a false sense of security.

When we have no control over our environment or experiences as a minor child, where do we turn for a sense of normalcy or security? The only way I can think of is to create an ideal life in our dream world. We cannot escape what is, and there are those times we have no choice but to deal with it. At least we can escape to our other world on occasion. Those who say dreams can never come true, or there are no such things as miracles, must be the most hopeless of all—with no vision of a brighter future to keep them going.

REFLECTIONS

Each man controls his own destiny
in this world. It doesn't matter how
much guidance and counseling he
receives along the way; he directs his
own life in the end.

Man succumbs to his own instincts;
Oftentimes disregarding the warnings
and sound advice he has been given.

A common pitfall to humanity is
that we must experience everything
ourselves and do it *"our way,"* even
if the risk is great, and many before
have fallen prey to this destructive
force. Reasoning, common sense,
and objectivity are somewhere lost, and
emotionality and irrational acts
take over.

The young think they have plenty
of time to gamble with their lives.
If things don't work out they can
follow another another course. Unfortunately,
sometimes that *special plum* is
offered only once, and can never be
recovered. They must then grasp at
what they can and be reconciled to
accepting second best, or mediocrity,
instead of greatness.

"MISCELLANEOUS MEANDERINGS"

The vicissitudes of human
nature give rise to many
thoughts and questions.

Pet peeves can prompt
us to action--either
passive, as in written form,
or active, as in retaliation.

MELODY AND RHYME

Poetry, in and of itself, is a musical expression of language. Following a rhythmic cadence, it is not surprising that it readily lends itself to a melody.

Sometimes familiar tunes aptly follow the ebb and flow of words. Other times, a melody generates from the mind of the poet.

Verse expressed in song tends to linger in the memory long after spoken or oral renderings have fled.

Let there be music!

WORLD OF MUSIC

Music is a way of life
For many in our world.
Rhythm, tempo are a part
Of music scores unfurled.

Major, minor, set a mood;
The classics never die;
Other songs will drift away—
They're gone, just like a sigh.

Melodies float through the air
As tones bombard our ears;
Spirits lift as songs burst forth
And pristine silence sheers.

Pity for the tone deaf ones
For whom sound has no tone.
 Blessed are those who have an ear
To synthesize a tune.

MUSIC

Music, music fills the air.
Music, music, everywhere.
Music in the world around
Bombards senses with its sound.

Sense the rhythm; feel the beat;
One can't help but tap his feet.
Floating melodies abound,
Coupled with harmonic sound.

Motion and emotion teem;
Sending out a ra'dient beam.
Instrumentals add appeal,
Giving textures we can feel.

Practice list'ning to the tunes—
A collection for our runes.
Self expression is the aim
Music helps us to attain.

A LITERARY TURN

Reading for pleasure,
Reading to learn,
Picking a genre—
Where does one turn?

Fiction? Non-fiction?
Poe'try or prose?
What is your pleasure?
Books—rows on rows.

Nature or mys'try?
Biography?
Tragedy? Humor?
Philosophy?

Paperback? Hardbound?
Choose what you will,
Print style's important,
  So's writer's skill.

So many choices
Rattle the mind,
Explore all there is—
Discover and find.

Library, bookstore,
Most anywhere,
Reading material—
Buy it or share.

VISION

I could not see the blackboard,
The flashcards were not clear,
I sat close to the TV,
The eye chart was a blur.

The school nurse called my mother,
Reported what she found,
A trip to the eye doctor
Was scheduled right away.

The office was imposing.
What were these strange machines?
They looked like alien monsters—
I wondered if they hurt?

Relieved I was soon after,
For no pain did I feel;
The images came clearer
As lenses fell in place.

Hurrah, the test is over,
And now the fun can start,
It's time to pick a glass frame,
Oh where should I begin?

When once the frames are chosen,
Impatiently I wait,
At last the telephone rings—
My glasses have arrived.

And now I see a new world,
I see a blade of grass,
I see so sharp and clearly,
What wonders I behold.

RETIREMENT

We welcome the day...
Retirement's near;
The years that we worked
Are ended right here.

A sense of purpose,
A new set of mind
Can lead us onward
To uncharted find.

Beware of the rut
Of daily malaise;
Routines that threaten
To dampen our blaze.

Enjoy our freedom...
Hard-earned, it's our due.
Let's make each day count...
To self always true.

CONVENTION MANIA

Convention time is near,
The parties rally round
To back their candidates
Of whom they are so proud.

Unblemished records bared,
Their qualities unfold
Their right to represent
Constituents' intent.

The speeches stimulate
Support from near and far,
Enthusiasm roused
To greet this rising star.

Emotions run amok
When fueled by the mob,
Douse chaos by the horde,
Let order be restored.

May silence rule the tongues
And open up the ears,
So all may be informed,
Evaluate their peers.

JUSTICE

What is justice?
Who can tell?
For some, it sounds
The dread death knell.

For other souls
Hope springs anew,
When a future
They can view.

For some there comes
A prison term;
A judge and jury
Rule stands firm.

Do we punish
Or defend...
Achieving justice
In the end?

Is justice in
A court of law?
Revenge for deeds?
Yet there's a flaw!

Avenge oneself,
Is that the way
To mete out justice?
Who can say?

In all of us
An evil lurks.
Who's so perfect...
Has no quirks?

Am I the one
To say what's right?
Are you a judge...
Telling black from white?

What is justice?
Can you tell?
It's not so easy
To know what befell.

FLAME FURIES

The flickering flames
Search ever skyward,
Devouring all things
That lie in their path.

The vengeance of fire
Shows mercy to no one,
It quickly lays waste
To that which would thwart it.

The heat radiates,
It scorches and burns;
The fire rages on,
New vistas to conquer.

The beauty of fire
Belies its intention,
Destruction is foremost,
It must be contained.

When flames slowly die,
Relinquish their power,
The embers and ashes
In silence await.

MUSHY, CRUNCHY

I like mushy,
I like crunchy,
Mushy branflakes,
Crunchy cornflakes.

I like mushy,
I like crunchy,
Mushy melons,
Crunchy apples.

I like mushy,
I like crunchy,
Mushy choc'late,
Crunchy crackers.

I like mushy,
I like crunchy,
Mushy grahams,
Crunchy pretzels.

Mushy, crunchy,
Such a contrast,
Paradox of
Choice and pre'frence.

A LIE

PRINTED IN THE NIGHT SKY (1993)
THE NATIONAL LIBRARY OF POETRY
AND
POETIC VOICES OF AMERICA (SPRING, 1998)
SPARROWGRASS POETRY FORUM

A lie starts out a little thing---
A word or two gone wrong.
Before you know, it multiplies,
And binds you like a thong.

What first prompts that slip of tongue---
That leads you to deep water
From which you find you can't escape?
Let's warn your sons and daughters!

A lie seems unimportant first,
Like stepping on quicksand,
You're unaware 'til it's too late
To reach a helping hand.

One lie leads to another;
The truth falls far behind,
Losing sight of what is fact---
It does confuse the mind!

When once a lie is spoken
It's like a rolling stone---
Picking up debris and trash,
It builds into a mountain.

So let that be a lesson learned---
Think before you utter,
Lest you get caught up in a lie,
From which you'll ne'er recover.

COMPROMISE

World is changing,
Quick fix on,
Quality sacrificed,
Quantity gained.

Family structure
Drastically altered,
Pressure from peers
Crushes our ethics,
Values adopted
By popular vote.

Morals dissolve,
That we be accepted,
Appetites sexual
Demand satisfaction,
Forcing young girls
To yield or defy.

Cruelty reigns,
Honor has fallen
Victim to masses...
Who dares to arise?

LURE OF A HARLEY
BY ELAINE MARTIN UONELLI

A Harley...a Harley,
The shouts ring o'er the land;
Where to find a Harley?
They're always in demand.

This well known bike is mint,
Expensive taste have those
Looking through the showroom,
Which model have they chose?

Selection fin'ly made,
Accessories to add,
Customize their choice,
How elegantly clad.

The Harley is unique,
Magical its power,
Luring avid bikers,
Appealing to the bold.

A man becomes a boy,
A boy becomes a man,
Riding on a Harley
He's ruler of the land.

LONGEVITY—A BLESSING OR A CURSE?

As I was growing up, our youth group often visited nursing homes in an effort to spread some cheer, and to let the people know God loved them and hadn't forgotten them. Many of the residents seemed to look forward to our programs and visits. In those days, the conditions were not the best, and you needed a perfumed hanky under your nose. The body odors and smells of urine and excrement were overwhelming.

Great advances have been made in terms of odor control. Even security measures have been installed to contain those who would wander off. The facility, in general, is more esthetic—no doubt to assuage the guilt of the caregiver who has left his loved one here to gradually waste away in body and spirit.

My mother held to the opinion that when you didn't want to be bothered with a troublesome parent, you shucked him away in a nursing home.

Today, I know, "If you live long enough, you will end up in a nursing home." Why should this be true if you have family or friends who care about you?

Caregivers, be they family or friends, can only continue as long as their own physical and mental health endure. Inevitably, the object of their concern becomes increasingly demanding as physical needs increase and mental faculties diminish to the point that the loved one is no longer capable of directing his own actions. The caregiver is unable to cope with the increased responsibilities on a nonstop, 25-hour a day basis and maintain his own sanity: ergo, enter, the nursing home.

As long as we can be more or less self-sufficient, with just an occasional helping hand, life is good. Unfortunately, those additional years begin to take their toll—we may be affected physically, mentally, or both.

When you visit a nursing home, you witness numerous aspects of disabilities. Chronological ages vary widely, as do mental ages; however, you meet more 75+ people than those who are younger.

The individual with any degree of conscious awareness welcomes visitors. Sometimes his conversations are rational, and other times he rambles— confused as to time, place, and who he is.

Characteristics are as varied as a rainbow's hues. You meet folks who are shy and reticent or, in sharp contrast, antagonistic and belligerent. There are those who reject assistance and those who plead for help.

You see despair, fear, and confusion. You also see withdrawal, silence, and the appearance of a quiescent attitude. Who knows what rages in the minds of the quiet ones? Those who are vocal in their complaints and aggressive in their behavior are able to vent some of their frustration.

Loneliness encompasses all like a fog—no matter how much life stirs around them. Each and every person lives in his own private hell. There may be a haven in the minds of a few, but it seems to be rare.

God bless those who devote their lives to caring for this most diverse, and many times difficult population.

COMPLACENCY

Things we take for granted,
Learning as we grow,
Starting with our senses,
How many do you know?

Smell detects what's rotten—
Pleasant odors too;
Sight reveals what's ugly—
Also colors' hue.

Sound impinges eardrums—
Volume, pitch, and tone
Binds us to surroundings,
People, self, and home.

Taste remains in mem'ry
After food's imbibed—
Sour, salty, bitter,
Sweet tastes—all are tried.

Touch is kinesthetic,
Many clues it yields,
Temp'rature and texture
Heighten what we feel.

Modern ways of living
Move along so fast—
Time out for reflection,
Mind those things that last.

KEEP IN STEP

Feet...feet...pick up your feet—
One right after the other.
Feet...feet...pick up your feet—
Lest you stumble and fall.

Feet...feet...pick up your feet—
Keep the pace regulated.
Feet...feet...pick up your feet—
Feel the rhythmic beat.

Breathe...breathe...in and out—
Take your time, do not hurry.
Time...time...plenty of time—
To do what you have to do.

Dedicated to unmindful hurriers.

WHO LIKES.........

Who likes watching good movies,
Reading a book,
Classical music,
A happy look?

Who likes frost-covered windows,
Bright, starry nights,
Sitting 'round campfires,
Colorful lights?

Who likes sweet smelling flowers,
Choc'late with nuts,
Smells in a bak'ry,
Kittens and mutts?

Who likes winning a contest,
Not being shoved,
Steamy hot showers,
Feeling you're loved?

Who likes talking with people,
Vacationing,
Sleeping when tired,
Happy endings?

WHO HATES.....

Who hates freezing cold weather,
Skidding on ice,
Driving in traffic
Heads full of lice?

Who hates cleaning the windows,
Cluttered up drawers,
Lightning and thunder,
When the wind roars?

Who hates examinations,
Having to cram,
Going on diets,
Liver and lamb?

Who hates rudeness in people,
Racing the clock,
Balancing checkbooks,
Getting a shock?

Who hates biting mosquitoes,
Insects and bugs,
Boa constrictors,
Slow, slimy slugs?

Who hates people who argue,
Blood-curdling tales,
Misunderstandings,
Trimming dogs' nails?

Who hates sinking in quicksand,
Being afraid,
Rooms filled with smoke,
Not being paid?

Who hates climbing a mountain,
Steep heights and depths,
Getting up early,
Sickness and death?

EXERCISE IN ACTION

Want to get your body
Fit and into shape?
Hurry into CURVES now,
Come on, keep that date.

Exercise is vital,
Lest you gather dust,
Structure gives you balance,
Routine is a must.

Stepping keeps up heart rate,
Movements are not crude,
Rhythm helps the action,
Music maintains mood.

Breathing is essential,
Consciously control,
Inhale, exhale slowly,
Regulate blood flow.

Clothes should not be binding,
Tennis shoes are best,
Clockwise is the pattern,
Now to take a rest.

Listen to your mentors,
Lest you should get lax,
Stretching ends the session,
Muscles can relax.

INSPIRATION

I looked for inspiration...
Inspiration found I none.
And, then, at last, unbidden,
Inspiration---it did come.

Was it buried or suppressed?
Was it hidden or denied?
Then it shone forth, bright as day;
Don't let it be denied!

Inspiration comes from where?
To us, a mystery.
Yet, when it comes, it opens eyes;
It sets our spirits free.

Perhaps it was a babe's first first cry...
Roused dormant thoughts long buried.
Or when a bird takes to the sky...
Ideas formed are varied.

Was it someone met today?
A scented flower's bloom?
A special word or deed from one...
Who freed our thoughts from doom?

Inspiration, let it flow;
Don't bank it up inside.
Let the well spring open wide,
And ride upon the tide.

THE RIDE

She got into her '77 Caddy, her trusty chariot of steel. Confident of a successful ride, she pulled slowly out of her stall, mindful of quiescent stable-mates around her.

Veering around the corner, she lost control of her horses. Her eyes, two fireflies darting through the gloom, sought a safe harbor. An empty stall loomed before her. She headed for the vacuum and the concrete barrier that would impede her flight.

But no, her horses had enough momentum and power to carry her over the wall.

Her glassy eyes beheld the yawning abyss before her. Could she survive a headlong journey down the treacherous slopes, avoiding alien rocks and unfathomable pits?

She was like a ship at sea—buffeted by angry waves determined to upend her craft.

Relentlessly her horses pulled her onward. A dark, forbidding obstacle stood in her path. As she steered toward the telephone pole, her capricious chariot came to a halt.

WEATHER WOES

Springtime floods can be destructive,
Overflowing farm and field,
Light'ning strikes without distinction,
Havoc wrought that will not yield.

Summer heat, humidity,
Cooling fans and breeze we crave,
Droughts and insects plague the land,
Crops and plants we strive to save.

Autumn brings capricious whims,
Watch out for the falling limbs,
Avalanches and mudslides
Devastate the countryside.

Winter blizzards, freezing frosts,
Icy highways—traction lost,
Chilled through body, reddened nose,
Frozen fingers, benumbed toes.

Twisters, cyclones, hurricanes,
Sandstorms, windstorms, tidal waves,
Angry winds unleash their fury,
Ruthless, they dispense their rage.

Earthquakes open fissures wide,
Leaving man no place to hide,
Ashes fall and lava flows
From volcanoes wakened, bold.

Mother Nature claims the world,
Shows no mercy, deeds unfurl.
Never satisfied, we pine
　For the perfect, ideal clime.

IT'S A CONSPIRACY...
A WOMAN'S LAMENT

It's a conspiracy! What have we done
  To deserve such a fate...A destiny won?
It might be our father, or our brother;
  It might be a husband, or a lover.

What could be their intent?
  These men in our lives,
Who riddle us with guilt,
  Sharp as any knives.

They want model women;
  Someone to share with them,
Someone who's there.
  Their ears are for others,

Not tuned to their own;
  What maketh our voice heard?
To us needs be shown.
  For try as we might

To be understood,
  We're heard, but not heeded...
As if we were wood.
  They have double standards

We can't understand;
  They're sitting in judgement
All over the land.
  Women libbers cry out,

They want justice for all.
  Come, give us your ear now...
Give heed to our call.

We are not asking
   For what we've not earned;
Nor are we demanding...
   Have you listened and learned?

We don't want your pity;
   Understanding we crave;
Sensitivity,too,
   Lest we go to our grave---

Frustrated, heart-broken;
   Our men do not hear.
Our thoughts go unspoken;
   Oh,where is their ear?

Our needs are so simple;
   Desires are so few...
Assurance we're loved;
   Please let it be true!

Driven to the brink
   Of madness and despair...
All for just one sign,
   One sign you truly care.

Do we ask too much?
   Is it so hard to give
Your reassurance,
   That we might cope and live?

So easily we're crushed
   By a word or a deed,
Don't take us for granted,
   For we fill a need...

A balance in nature,
   To rule and be ruled;
A man and a woman,
   Now heated, now cooled.

COMMUNICATE

Communicate! Communicate!
Communication is—
A two-way street.

Listen well,
Think it through,
Choose your words most carefully.

Articulate your sounds,
Enunciate your words,
It's not always easy—
But well worth the effort,

And you will be successful,
You'll hear, and be heard.

OF SHOES AND SHIPS AND POLITICS

When in polite society,
Some topics we avoid—
Religion, sex, and politics
Are subjects that annoy.

Unless like-minded is the crowd,
Discussion is taboo,
Republicans and Democrats,
And Independents, too...

Conservatives and Liberals,
None share a point of view;
Each party stands for what is right,
For what is just and true.
From their perspective, long thought out,
Diversities accrue.

On issues—some—they may agree,
The vote may be the same,
Solutions seldom follow suit,
Oh, who or what to blame?

Democracy's the way to go
When all is said and done;
The check and balance way of life
Discourages the gun.

Republicans and Democrats
And Independents—all
Must learn to compromise at times,
Lest our great nation fall.

SOULS IN TORMENT

Swimming in a dead pool—
Floundering, sinking.
Striving to keep afloat—
Flailing, choking.

Tortured soul in anguish,
Beating at the bars,
Dark'ning world closing in—
Crushing, over-whelming.

Pursued by vengeful demons,
Betrayed, abused
By those we trust,
Besieged by pain and loss,
Sorrow breaks the bough.

Lost and searching for a life,
Salvation not in sight,
Yesterdays become tomorrows,
Plundered spirit seeks release.

FLUENCY

Fluency is a rhythm.
Fluency is a rhyme.
Fluency's cadence
Is a state of mind.

Unruffled like a pond;
Smooth flowing as a lake;
Gliding o'er the frozen ice,
With each breath we take.

Uninterrupted stream;
Forward movement—glide.
Striding ever onward;
Going with the tide.

Reflected sunlight radiates.
Luminous moonbeams glow.
Imagination stretches
As fluent patterns grow.

As we perceive—
So are we.

Dedicated to the disfluent among us

A GOLDWING ADVENTURE

It's time, it's time
To mount our wing
And leave behind
The mundane chores.

Look up ahead,
The highway calls;
Perhaps a bump
Along the way.

But worth it all---
Consider this
No time or space
Can hold us now.

For we are free,
The weather's fine,
To ride and ride---
Enjoy the view.

A myraid
Of sights
and sounds,
Of smells and feels---

That overwhelm
Our minds
And stir
Fine tuned senses.

A TRADITIONAL VIEW OF CHRISTMAS

Christmas cookies baking,
Spice scents everywhere,
Pine trees loose their fragrance,
Permeate the air.

Church bells gaily ringing
In the frosty night,
Carolers singing sweetly
Dressed in blue and white.

Brilliant, sparkling snowflakes
Fill the ev'ning skies,
Flames leap up from fires
Bringing tears to eyes.

Multi-colored papers
Wrap the many gifts
Placed beneath the fir tree,
Hidden by the drifts.

Silence reigns in darkness,
Broken when it's light,
Joyous voices welcome
Christmas Day so bright.

MESSAGE FROM A FLOWER

Flowers in a garden;
Flowers growing wild;
Watch them flourish daily,
Colorful and mild.

Flowers on a table;
Flowers in a yard;
Flowers by a bedside;
Flowers on a card.

Flowers full of fragrance;
Flowers without scent;
Each one has its value;
Each one's only lent.

Essence of a flower
Often is released
By unwary trampling---
Crushed beneath our feet.

Flowers aren't forever,
Life on earth is short;
Memories are lasting;
Time alone can sort.

Flowers on a birthday
Celebrate a birth.
Flowers from a loved one
Indicate one's worth.

Accolades with flowers
Honor acts and deeds.
Graduation flowers
Proclaim learn'ed deeds.

Flowers for a gala
Add a touch of class.
Flowers at a wedding
Beautify the mass.

Flowers at a grave side
Mourn the loss of life.
Resurrection flowers
Praise the end of strife.

SONG FOR THE ROAD

Rollin', rollin', rollin'—
Keep those wheels a-rollin',
Keep that chassis goin'—
Roll on—roll on.

No matter what the weather,
We must keep on together,
Roll on—roll on.

Check the tires, check the brakes,
Check the choke, check the lights,
Check the fuel, check the oil, roll on.

Watch your speed, watch the signs,
Watch the road, watch for cars,
Watch the ditch, watch the bump, roll on.

Look ahead—off the road,
See that sign? What's it say?
Don't you know? It's MacDonalds!

Time to stop, time to rest,
Time for burgers, time for fries,
And don't forget the milkshake!

LEAFY BALLET

Released from their bonds,
Restraints have they none,
The dancers prepare—
Empow'rd by the wind.

The street is the stage,
Performance unique,
Capricious and wild,
Ballet now begins.

So graceful the steps,
The intricate moves,
The style and the form
Entrance all who view.

They whirl and they twirl,
And leap toward the sky,
Returning to earth,
Pursuing the dance.

Bereft of their leaves,
The old stately trees
An audience form
For leafy ballets.

THE STORM

A once gentle breeze
Turns into a gale.
A once darkened sky
Illumined in light.
A once silent night
The thunder does pierce.
A once light rainfall
Becomes a downpour.

A quiescent time
Is rent with a roar
Of sound now unleashed.
A complacent life
Seeks shelter from storm.

At last it is spent,
This vengeful wild force.
A gradual return
To calm and to rest.
The mayhem winds wrought
Disturbed nature's plan.

PROCRASTINATION

Procrastination is a fault
I fight most everyday.
Tomorrow's promise beckons me
I know today can wait.

I look around and am amazed
At all there is to do.
But can't it wait another time?
My energy is drained.

Complacent now, I've found excuse
To put off pressing chores,
Because I know tomorrow's near—
Forget about today.

TECHNOLOGICALLY CHALLENGED

The school grades were all passing;
No problem with the tests;
A graduation followed;
 It's time to take a rest.

In high school and in college,
Computers not yet in,
Success was not a problem—
With study one could win.

The world today is changing;
Machines now rule the day;
Computers taking over
What once was man's domain.

The young may have no problem;
They know no other way;
Now oldsters in the workplace
Have lost out without pay.

If they reject the new ways,
Another job must find,
Alas, the resumé now
Requires a P.C. mind.

The myst'ry of computers
Evades the nat'ral mind,
Confounds the wise among us,
And humbles those behind.

SCHOOL DAZE

Nineteen hundred fifty-nine
From hallowed halls of ivy,
A class superb you won't forget—
We were so very lively.

Our academics were foremost,
With sports not far behind;
Achievement in dramatics gained,
Our match is hard to find.

Capricious pranks were not amiss
When from the bold and brave.
The serious minded looked in awe,
Their dignity to save.

Though we are no way biased,
We really must admit,
That when compared to other years,
We surely had true grit!

NIGHT VS. DAY

I married an owl;
I married a bat;
I married a man
Who shuns all daylight.

When others are up
And do normal things,
Oh where is he then?
Asleep in the bed!

The curtains are drawn
Lest light filter in
Disturbing the sleep
That he does desire.

As midnight arrives,
He stirs from his rest;
He's ready to join
His comrades in time.

There's no compromise,
It's his way or none;
Prepare for the ride,
Or be left behind.

Avoiding the guilt
Of staying at home,
I put on my clothes
And yield to his call.

DEPRESSION

Depression is a malady,
Tenacious is its hold;
It strips away our self-esteem,
Depletes our reservoirs.

A merciless attack on all,
Denigrates all who yield,
Discourages a happy thought,
Demoralizes man.

Insidious, it wears away,
Attacks sub-conscious minds
To follow its destructive path
That leads to blackest hell.

Encourages dependency
On pharmaceuticals—
A false sense of security
That robs our self control.

Beware the web depression spins
To trap unwary souls;
Stand strong against its siren song—
To dash us 'gainst the shoals.

A TALE TO BE TOLD

If a tire could talk,
A tale might be told
Of many long miles
It traveled the road.

Brand new is the car,
The treads are all fresh,
Smell of new rubber,
Passed all the road tests.

Inflated with air,
White sidewalls a-gleam,
The matte of black tire—
No pinpricks are seen.

As year follows year,
The rubber's worn thin,
A stray piece of glass
Caused tire to spin.

Control now is lost
As rubber is shed,
Entrails are left—
Remains of the dead.

Auspicious its start,
Degraded its end,
Shredded, discarded,
With naught left to mend.

THE GIFT

Phyllis Teague she had a doll—
A genuine Zapf baby.
She was.. oh so sweet.
She was.. oh so dear.
She was.. oh so real,
And now her name is Laura.

There came a day when Aunt Phyl said,
"I want to share my baby—
With a niece of mine,
Who I know is kind,
Who I know will care,
And love my precious baby."

THE SEARCH

You never know what you will find
Until you start to look;
The treasures in an old junkyard
You won't find in a book.

Among chaotic, rusting ruins
You might find what you need.
The inventory may not show,
You must go forth and heed—

The clues that all around you lie.
Investigate the wrecks;
Be vigilant, with eyes alert,
And clear away the decks.

"Eureka," now you shout aloud,
"See what I just uncovered—
That missing part for which I've searched
I now have just discovered."

A STATE OF MIND

Monotony and ennui
We glean from repetition.
Our senses dull, our spirits lull,
We sink beneath tradition.

Complacency and apathy
Accompany routine pathways.
Less energy and lethargy
Perpetuate our mind haze.

Consistency, stability,
A sense of peace we get;
Now add predictability,
Perpetuate our mind-set.

Variety, diversity,
A pinch of moderation,
Two drops of spontaneity
Complete the infiltration.

PATIENCE

Patience, patience—
  This is what we need.
Patience, patience—
  If we would succeed.

Patience is a virtue, it's true.
We must have patience
If we'd do what we have to do.

Patience, patience—
  It doesn't hurt to wait;
Rewards may come
  To those who hesitate.

If we have patience,
  We won't regret
The time spent waiting
Can pay off yet.

Inspired by observing humanity's
impatience on the highway.

WHAT IS TRUTH?

What is truth?
Stranger than fiction.
Is it fact,
Or supposition?

What is truth?
Can it be measured?
What is real?
Something to treasure.

Who to trust?
What can we believe?
No one knows.
Some try to deceive.

What is truth?
You must be the judge,
As life's path
We all have to trudge.

BATTLEFRONT

The sun beats down upon the earth,
The yard is filled with untamed weeds.

An ice bag cools a sweating brow,
The mower strains against impasse.

United front—
The weeds resist relentless blades.

Undaunted now—
Sweep through the ranks.

Persistence pays—
The lawn is mowed at last.

BREAKABLE

I'm posturing before the world...
Hiding self from view,
Protecting 'gainst intrusions rude,
Dammed up tears behind eyelids.

Conforming to what is expected,
Emotions jailed,
Dare not expose,
Eggshell fragile, lightly tread.
Jealous guarding sacred shrine,
No admittance to this realm.

Inner demons sear my soul,
A glimpse into my private hell,
Destructive thoughts arise unbidden,
Assail my conscious mind,
I find myself cast into limbo,
Adrift—no place to moor,
Dark solitude crowds 'round me,
Steals my very breath,
Leaves no room for comfort,
Alone I fight the beast.

Restore my equilibrium,
My prayers ascend to heaven,
Directed to another's voice
That strengthens my resolves—
Tenuous hold on life.

Treasured friends are hov'ring near—
Offering empathy.

Be ye Irish,
Or be ye not,
St. Patrick's Day
Can mean a lot.

Filled pots of gold,
And shamrocks green,
The leprechauns—
What do they mean?

A fact or myth,
The tales of yore?
The magic clings
To our heart's core.

So celebrate
Along with me,
Let's all wear green,
And Irish be.

IRISH AT HEART!

ACCOUNTABILITY

Have you ever heard
Of a 5-minute job,
The wisdom of they,
Long stories made short?

Have you ever heard
Of laws that aren't broken,
A promise not kept,
A question unanswered?

Have you ever heard
Vows made 'twixt two lovers—
For better or worse,
'Til death do us part?

Words oft are spoken
Unthinking and glib;
Deeds oft committed
Without conscious thought.

Remember that actions
Speak louder than words,
And words that are spoken
Can ne'er be recalled.

TRAVELING

Highway, byway—	Keeping up your speed,
Highway, byway—	All the signs you heed.
Highway, byway—	Looking out for bumps,
Highway, byway—	Don't hit any stumps.
Highway, byway—	Eyes on the alert,
Highway, byway—	Don't with danger flirt.
Highway, byway—	Traffic stopped ahead,
Highway, byway—	Roadwork stops you dead.
Highway, byway—	On the move again,
Highway, byway—	Traffic signals send.
Highway, byway—	Potholes in the road,
Highway, byway—	Time to shift your load.
Highway, byway—	Road is mesmerizing,
Highway, byway—	Fixated your eyes,
Highway, byway—	Fight to keep awake,
Highway, byway—	Human life at stake.
Highway, byway—	Obstacles all breached,

SEXUALITY

Progression of our sexuality,
Phases that it must go through,
Beginning with our latent tendencies,
Born to follow and pursue.

Developing a gender preference,
Male and female are the norm...
Acknowledge and respect diversities,
Morals, ethics, all are formed.

Environment, associations
Shape us, make us what we are,
DNA, heredity...
Are the building blocks.

Like a seed requiring nourishment...
Sunlight, water...help it grow.
Love, encouragement, guidance, structure...
Ingredients that make us whole.

STRICKEN

Headache, sore throat,
The muscles creak and groan.
Eyes and nose run—
The symptoms are full-blown.

Tissues, cough drops—
A cold bug strikes the weak.
Self treat? Doctor?
The quickest cure we seek.

Lots of water,
To bed, to bed and rest.
Meds and as'prin—
This cold is such a pest!

Time and patience
Are practices that cure.
Symptoms gone now—
Renewed and health insured.

A POET'S PSYCHE

Poets are people
Who bare their own souls;
They let words unwind
From spools in their mind.

Recognition and cognition
Of ideas in the brain,
Harbored in the space of mem'ry,
Can no longer be restrained.

Unbound, free—they now are floating,
Random thoughts that fill the air
Must be captured, written down—
Quickly—ere the words are gone.

Stories spin out
On gossamer threads—
All woven into
A fabric of hue.

Pastels and vibrants—
Some muted, some bold,
Swirl over the page—
None fitting a mold.

Nat'ral functions interrupted,
Sleeping, waking, all disturbed
'Til the process is completed—
Poe'try banners are unfurled.

Rejoice!

Without pain there's no sense of relief.
Without loss there's no sense of gain.
Without depression there's no sense of joy.
Without testing patience can't grow.
Adversity seasons us.

Flee the daily stress and strife,
Leave behind your pain and toil,
Be not consumed by gloom and doom,
Let not yourself be dragged asunder.

Look for the pot of gold
At the rainbow's end.
Glory in the light
At the tunnel's end.

Raise your voice in celebration,
Absorb the warmth of caring friends,
Cling to happy memories,
And give thanks for each new day,

PEACE

Think about peace,
Read about peace,
Pray about peace,
Sing about peace,
And look for peace -
A passive peace.

Speak out for peace,
Cry out for peace,
March for peace,
Petition for peace,
And fight for peace-
Aggressive peace.

Is it in books?
Is it in minds?
Is it in words
Spoken aloud?

Where does it start?
Where does it end?
This search for peace-
Can it be found?
Oh, that we could
Omniscient be-
Engender peace
Throughout the world.

TRIBUTE TO A BUSINESS WOMAN

A business woman in this world
Has no easy life;
She must be tough, she must be firm,
Overcoming strife.

The men conspire to put her down,
Jealous are her peers;
The women envy her success—
They should break out in cheers.

Support another of their sex,
Lend a helping hand,
Admire the progress she has made,
Yield to her demands.

A business woman in this world
Stands Firm—is in control,
Is open to employees gripes,
Fair dealing is her goal.

Inspired by Marcella Singer

Elaine M. Uonelli, author of Fragments, considers reading and writing poetry therapy for the soul. She encourages her readers to pen their own poems if they have not already done so. Even if no one but your family and friends sees your efforts, the joy is in sharing feelings, thoughts, and ideas.

Ms. Uonelli suggests you read the verses aloud. Taste the language and flavor of rhythm and sound.